English
made easy

Key Stage 1
ages 6-7
Workbook 2

Author
Brenda Apsley

DK

LONDON • NEW YORK • SYDNEY • DELHI

The ie and oo sounds

Four spelling patterns make the same **ie** sound. They are:

ie as in p**ie**   **i_e** as in b**i**t**e**   **igh** as in h**igh**   **y** as in b**y**

Write a word to label each picture, then write another word with the same spelling pattern.

Remember: Different letter sets make the same sound.

k ....

....

....

....

Four spelling patterns make the same **oo** sound. They are:

oo as in s**oo**n   **u_e** as in c**u**t**e**   **ew** as in ch**ew**   **ue** as in bl**ue**

Write a word to label each picture, then write another word with the same spelling pattern.

....

....

....

....

The ai, ee and oa sounds

Three spelling patterns make the same **ai** sound. They are:

    ai as in t**ai**l   **ay** as in s**ay**   **a_e** as in n**a**m**e**

Write a word to label each picture, then write another word with the same spelling pattern.

Remember: Different letter sets make the same sound.

   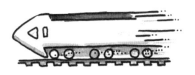   

. . . .

. . . .

Two spelling patterns make the same **ee** sound. They are:

    ee as in m**ee**t   **ea** as in m**ea**l

Write a word to label each picture, then write another word with the same spelling pattern.

. . . .

. . . .

Three spelling patterns make the same **oa** sound. They are:

    oa as in c**oa**t   **o_e** as in n**o**t**e**   **ow** as in r**ow**

Write a word to label each picture, then write another word with the same spelling pattern.

. . . .

. . . .

Handwriting joins

Use **joined handwriting** to write these sets of letters and words.

Remember: Do not lift your pencil off the paper (except to dot the letter i).

an .... in .... um ....

can .... main .... sum ....

Now use **joined handwriting** to write these sets of letters and words that join at the top.

Remember: Letters join in different ways.

ou .... wi .... oo ....

our .... win .... room ....

Write labels in **joined handwriting** for these pictures.

....

....

....

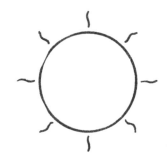

....

Handwriting joins

Use **joined handwriting** to write these sets of small letters joined to tall letters.

Remember: Small letters join to tall letters in different ways.

al   ....   el   ....   ul   ....

wh   ....   ot   ....   ut   ....

Now use **joined handwriting** to write these words.

mall   ....   tall   ....   out   ....

who   ....   met   ....   not   ....

Write labels in **joined handwriting** for these pictures.

....

Now write your own name in **joined handwriting**. Start with a **capital letter**.

Remember: Capitals do not join to small letters.

Rob   Ali

....

Jane   Nita   Jack   Sara

The **air** sound

Four spelling patterns make the same **air** sound. They are:

air as in f**air**   **are** as in c**are**   **ere** as in th**ere**   **ear** as in w**ear**

Read the words in the box below. They all have the **air** sound. Then write each word in the right set.

pair	there	share	wear
where	scare	hairy	bear

air words

.... Pair ....

.... hairy ....

are words

....

....

ere words

....

....

ear words

....

....

Some words that sound the same mean different things and are spelt in different ways. Read these pairs of words that sound the same. Choose one word from each pair and use it to finish the sentence.

bear	bare

This is a hairy ....

stares	stairs

The bear goes up the ....

wear	where

Which hat will the bear ....?

A poem to read

Read this **poem** about cats. It is by a **poet** called Eleanor Farjeon. A **poet** is a person who writes **poems**.

Cats

Cats sleep
Anywhere,
Any table,
Any chair,
Top of piano,
Window-ledge,
In the middle,
On the edge,
Open drawer,
Empty shoe,
Anybody's
Lap will do,
Fitted in a
Cardboard box,
In the cupboard
With your frocks –
Anywhere!
They don't care!
Cats sleep
Anywhere.

Write the words in the **poem** that have the **air** sound.

Remember: The same sounds sometimes have different spellings.

.... Care .... chair ....

Now write one more word with the **air** sound. ....

Syllables

Each beat or unit in a word is called a **syllable**.

Read out loud these words that have **1 syllable**.

cat   make   will

Read out loud these words that have **2 syllables**.
The words are split into **syllables**.

tea•pot   to•day   be•fore

Read out loud these words that have **3 syllables**.

di•no•saur   hol•i•day

Count the number of **syllables** in each word (it may help to clap your hands after each beat). Then fill in the **chart** by writing the number of **syllables** in the box.

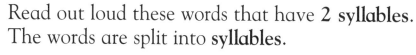

word	syllables
brother	2
begin	2
yesterday	3
another	3
purse	1
people	2
computer	2
mother	2

word	syllables
bedroom	2
always	2
football	2
boy	1
sister	2
family	3
because	2
father	2

A traditional story

Read this **story** from India, then answer the questions.

Alligator and Jackal

Jackal liked to eat crabs. So did Alligator, who was greedy. He wanted them all for himself.

One day Jackal went to the river to catch some crabs. But Alligator was waiting to catch him. Snap! went his big teeth on Jackal's paw.

Jackal played a trick on Alligator.

"Why are you eating a plant root?" he said.

"Am I?" said Alligator, opening his big mouth. Silly Alligator let Jackal go.

Alligator waited in the long grass to catch Jackal. But Jackal saw Alligator's tail moving the grass, and he ran away. Jackal escaped again.

Alligator found Jackal's den. But Jackal knew he had been there because he saw his claw marks in the soft mud.

When Alligator went to catch Jackal in his den, Jackal was ready for him. He lit a fire of sticks.

Alligator went into the den, but he soon ran out again. The thick smoke from Jackal's fire made him cough. It made him sneeze. It made his eyes water.

Alligator never tried to catch Jackal again. Clever Jackal! Now he could eat as many crabs as he liked.

Who was clever, Jackal or Alligator?

Jackal

Write a sentence about Jackal.

Jackal is very clever cunning

Write a sentence about Alligator.

Aligator is silly

useful words

> greedy
> slow
> clever
> fast
> silly

Dictionaries

A **dictionary** is a book of words.
A **dictionary** is a very useful book.
It helps you spell words.
It helps you find out what words mean.

Some **dictionaries** have pictures as well as words.

Words in **dictionaries** are in **alphabetical order**.
a b c d e f g h i j k l m n o p q r s t u v w x y z

Words that begin with the letter **a** are
at the **front** of the book.

Words that begin with the letter **z** are
at the **end** of the book.

lamb
A lamb is a baby sheep.

My
a to z
Book

Write words and draw pictures to fill in the gaps in these pages from
a **picture dictionary**.

chick

A chick is a baby hen.

lamb

a baby sheep

Kitten

A kitten is a baby cat.

Puppy

A puppy is a baby dog.

Definitions

This is a **dictionary page** of **c** words. The words are in thick, **bold** letters.

cage
A cage is something to keep small pets in.

calf
A calf is a baby cow.

canoe
A canoe is a small boat that you move with paddles.

cave
A cave is a large hole in the side of a hill or under the ground.

chair
A chair is something to sit on.

city
A city is a large town where lots of people live.

class
A class is a group of school children.

clock
A clock tells you what time it is.

Use the **dictionary page** above to help you fill in this **chart**.

word	meaning
city	A City A City is a place where a lot of people [people] live
A class	a group of school children
A calf	a baby cow
clock	A clock tells you the time.

The or sound

Five spelling patterns make the same **or** sound. They are:

or as in **for** **oor** as in **door** **ore** as in sto**re**
aw as in r**aw** **au** as in t**au**ght

Write the missing letters to finish each word below.
Then write the word on the line below.

Add **or** to these words.

sp_o__r_t

...... Sport ......

b_o__r_n

...... born ......

h_o__r_n

...... horn ......

Add **oor** to these words.

d_o__o__r_

...... door ......

fl_o__o__r_

...... Floor ......

p_o__o__r_

...... poor ......

Add **aw** to these words.

s_a__w_

...... Saw ......

p_a__w_

...... paw ......

dr_a__w_

...... draw ......

Add **au** to these words.

c_a__u_ght

...... Caught ......

n_a__u_ghty

...... naughty ......

d_a__u_ghter

...... daughter ......

Add **ore** to these words.

m_o__r__e_

...... more ......

t_o__r__e_

...... tore ......

s_o__r__e_

...... Sore ......

Compound words

Some words are made up of two other words. When two short words make one long word, the long word is called a **compound word**.

Try these word sums. Write the two words without a space between them to make one **compound word**, like this: **head** + **rest** = **headrest**.

lamp + post = *lamppost*

her + self = *herself*

milk + man = *milkman*

hand + bag = *handbag*

foot + stool = *footstool*

Draw lines to join up these **compound words**.

foot   card   play   bag

him   cake   school   man

post   ball   post   spoon

pan   self   tea   ground

Now write a list of the **compound words** that you joined above.

The er sound

Three spelling patterns make the same **er** sound. They are:

er as in h**er** **ir** as in s**ir** **ur** as in f**ur**

Read these **er** sound words out loud.

sir burn skirt her purse bird

turn girl hurt shirt curl were

Now write the **ir** words on the sh**ir**t. Write the **ur** words in the p**ur**se.

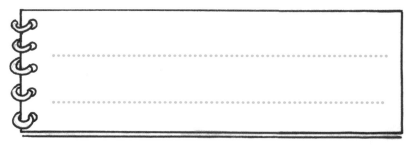

Write the **er** words on the list.

Write **er** sound words to label these pictures.

Remember: The same sounds are spelled in different ways.

Syllables

Write your **first name** here. Rebecca

How many **syllables** does your name have? three

Remember: Each beat or unit in a word is called a **syllable**.

Write the **names** below on the **chart**.

Tom ✓ Elizabeth ✓ Lee ✓ Natalie ✓ Edward ✓ Ben ✓ Alexander ✓
John ✓ Amber ✓ Mark ✓ Sita ✓ Tamara ✓ Jenny ✓ Kamal ✓ Sunita ✓

Remember: Names start with capital letters.

1 syllable	2 syllables
Tom Lee Ben Jhon Mark	Edward Amber sita Jenny Kamal

3 syllables	4 syllables
Natalie Tamara Sunita	Elizabeth Alexander

Now write the number of **syllables** in the **months** of the year.

January	4	April	2	July	2	October	3
February	4	May	1	August	2	November	3
March	1	June	1	September	3	December	3

A traditional story

Read this **traditional story** out loud.

Chicken Licken

One day an acorn fell out of a tree and hit Chicken Licken.
    "The sky is falling!" she said. "I must go and tell the king."
    "Where are you going?" asked Henny Penny.
    "The sky is falling," said Chicken Licken. "A piece of it fell on me. I am going to tell the king."
    "I will go with you," said Henny Penny.

    Chicken Licken and Henny Penny met Cocky Locky.
    "Where are you going?" asked Cocky Locky.
    "The sky is falling," said Henny Penny. "Chicken Licken told me."
    "A piece of it fell on me," said Chicken Licken.
    "I will go with you," said Cocky Locky.

    Chicken Licken, Henny Penny and Cocky Locky met Ducky Daddles.
    "Where are you going?" asked Ducky Daddles.
    "The sky is falling," said Cocky Locky. "Henny Penny told me."
    "Chicken Licken told me," said Henny Penny.
    "A piece of it fell on me," said Chicken Licken.
    "I will go with you," said Ducky Daddles.

    Chicken Licken, Henny Penny, Cocky Locky and Ducky Daddles met Goosey Loosey, Turkey Lurkey and Foxy Woxy, too.
    "Run into my house," said Foxy Woxy. "You will be safe there. I will tell the king for you."

What did Foxy Woxy do next? Write the end of the **story**.

There were foxs. They ate them all.

Now tell the **story** in your own words.

Answer Section with Parents' Notes

Key Stage 1
Ages 6–7
Workbook 2

This 8-page section provides answers or explanatory notes to all the activities in this book. This will enable you to assess your child's work.

Work through each page together, and ensure that your child understands each task. Point out any mistakes, and correct any handwriting errors. (Your child should use the handwriting style taught at his or her school.) As well as making corrections, it is very important to praise your child's efforts and achievements.

Encourage your child to develop the habit of using a word book or dictionary to find the meaning and correct spelling of a new word.

2

The ie and oo sounds

Four spelling patterns make the same ie sound. They are:
ie as in pie   i_e as in bite   igh as in high   y as in by

Write a word to label each picture, then write another word with the same spelling pattern.

Remember: Different letter sets make the same sound.

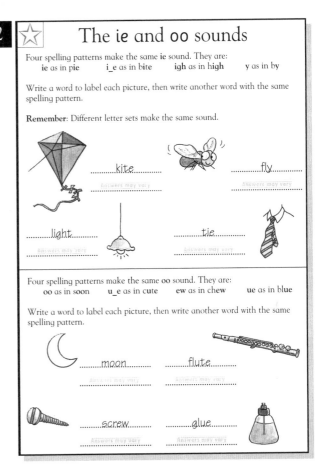

kite — Answers may vary
fly — Answers may vary
light — Answers may vary
tie — Answers may vary

Four spelling patterns make the same oo sound. They are:
oo as in soon   u_e as in cute   ew as in chew   ue as in blue

Write a word to label each picture, then write another word with the same spelling pattern.

moon — Answers may vary
flute — Answers may vary
screw — Answers may vary
glue — Answers may vary

This page looks at different spelling patterns that make the *ie* and *oo* sounds. Help your child to write a word for each picture, then develop the activity by asking him or her to write another word with the same pattern.

3

The ai, ee and oa sounds

Three spelling patterns make the same ai sound. They are:
ai as in tail   ay as in say   a_e as in name

Write a word to label each picture, then write another word with the same spelling pattern.

Remember: Different letter sets make the same sound.

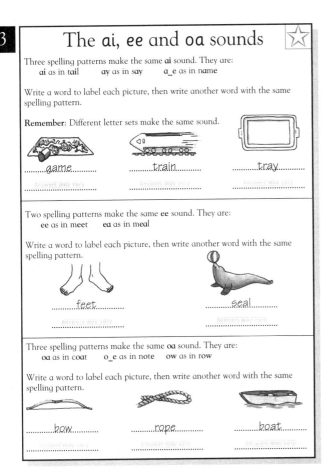

game — Answers may vary
train — Answers may vary
tray — Answers may vary

Two spelling patterns make the same ee sound. They are:
ee as in meet   ea as in meal

Write a word to label each picture, then write another word with the same spelling pattern.

feet — Answers may vary
seal — Answers may vary

Three spelling patterns make the same oa sound. They are:
oa as in coat   o_e as in note   ow as in row

Write a word to label each picture, then write another word with the same spelling pattern.

bow
rope
boat

Activities focusing on words with the same sounds but different spelling patterns will help your child to read and spell with confidence. After writing words to match the pictures, encourage your child to write other words with the same spelling patterns.

4

Handwriting joins

Use **joined handwriting** to write these sets of letters and words.

Remember: Do not lift your pencil off the paper (except to dot the letter i).

an   in   um
can   main   sum

Now use **joined handwriting** to write these sets of letters and words that join at the top.

Remember: Letters join in different ways.

ou   wi   oo
our   win   room

Write labels in **joined handwriting** for these pictures.

man   van
moon   sun

The first and second basic handwriting joins are diagonal and horizontal joins to letters without ascenders (parts that go above the body of the letter). Use the handwriting style that your child is being taught at school.

Handwriting joins

Use **joined handwriting** to write these sets of small letters joined to tall letters.

Remember: Small letters join to tall letters in different ways.

al .... el .... ul ....
wh .... ot .... ut ....

Now use **joined handwriting** to write these words.

mall .... tall .... out ....
who .... met .... not ....

Write labels in **joined handwriting** for these pictures.

................nut................ ....mat................ ....owl................

Now write your own name in **joined handwriting**. Start with a **capital letter**.

Remember: Capitals do not join to small letters.

Rob _____ Ali
Answers may vary
Jane   Nita   Jack   Sara

This page provides practice in writing fluently.
It looks at diagonal and horizontal joins to letters
with ascenders. Your child should also practise
writing names starting with capital letters, which
do not join.

The air sound

Four spelling patterns make the same **air** sound. They are:
air as in f**air**   **are** as in c**are**   **ere** as in th**ere**   **ear** as in w**ear**

Read the words in the box below. They all have the **air** sound. Then write
each word in the right set.

pair	there	share	wear
where	scare	hairy	bear

air words
........pair........
........hairy........

are words
........share........
........scare........

ere words
........there........
........where........

ear words
........wear........
........bear........

Some words that sound the same mean different things and are spelt in
different ways. Read these pairs of words that sound the same. Choose one
word from each pair and use it to finish the sentence.

bear   bare
This is a hairy ....bear........

stares   stairs
The bear goes up the ....stairs........

wear   where
Which hat will the bear ....wear........?

The activities on this page will help your child to
read and write words with the *air* sound that have
different spelling patterns. Your child needs to
know that words that sound the same can be spelt
in different ways and have different meanings.

A poem to read

Read this **poem** about cats. It is by a **poet** called Eleanor Farjeon. A **poet** is
a person who writes **poems**.

Cats

Cats sleep
Anywhere,
Any table,
Any chair,
Top of piano,
Window-ledge,
In the middle,
On the edge,
Open drawer,
Empty shoe,
Anybody's
Lap will do,
Fitted in a
Cardboard box,
In the cupboard
With your frocks –
Anywhere!
They don't care!
Cats sleep
Anywhere.

Write the words in the **poem** that have the **air** sound.

Remember: The same sounds sometimes have different spellings.
........anywhere........ ....chair........ ....care........
Now write one more word with the **air** sound. .... Answers may vary

Your child will enjoy reading this poem aloud. Talk
about poetry together, and explain the meaning of
words such as *verse*, *poem*, *poet* and *rhyme*. The
writing activity builds on the exercises on the
previous page, which investigate the *air* sound.

Syllables

Each beat or unit in a word is called a **syllable**.

Read out loud these words that have **1 syllable**.
cat   make   will

Read out loud these words that have **2 syllables**.
The words are split into **syllables**.
tea·pot   to·day   be·fore

Read out loud these words that have **3 syllables**.
di·no·saur   hol·i·day

Count the number of **syllables** in each word (it may help to clap your hands after
each beat). Then fill in the **chart** by writing the number of **syllables** in the box.

word	syllables
brother	2
begin	2
yesterday	3
another	3
purse	1
people	2
computer	3
mother	2

word	syllables
bedroom	2
always	2
football	2
boy	1
sister	2
family	3
because	2
father	2

Your child needs to recognise syllables and be able
to split words into syllables. Help him or her by
saying the words out loud, breaking them into
syllables and pausing between each one. Make the
activity fun by clapping along with each syllable.

A traditional story

Read this **story** from India, then answer the questions.

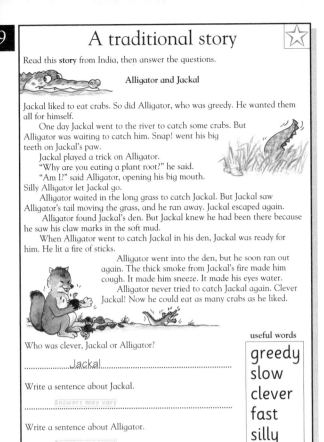

Alligator and Jackal

Jackal liked to eat crabs. So did Alligator, who was greedy. He wanted them all for himself.

One day Jackal went to the river to catch some crabs. But Alligator was waiting to catch him. Snap! went his big teeth on Jackal's paw.

Jackal played a trick on Alligator.

"Why are you eating a plant root?" he said.

"Am I?" said Alligator, opening his big mouth. Silly Alligator let Jackal go.

Alligator waited in the long grass to catch Jackal. But Jackal saw Alligator's tail moving the grass, and he ran away. Jackal escaped again.

Alligator found Jackal's den. But Jackal knew he had been there because he saw his claw marks in the soft mud.

When Alligator went to catch Jackal in his den, Jackal was ready for him. He lit a fire of sticks.

Alligator went into the den, but he soon ran out again. The thick smoke from Jackal's fire made him cough. It made him sneeze. It made his eyes water.

Alligator never tried to catch Jackal again. Clever Jackal! Now he could eat as many crabs as he liked.

useful words

greedy
slow
clever
fast
silly

Who was clever, Jackal or Alligator?

..............Jackal...............

Write a sentence about Jackal.

..............Answers may vary...............

Write a sentence about Alligator.

..............Answers may vary...............

Read this traditional story with your child. Confident readers will be able to read parts or all of it independently. Help your child to take information from the text to answer the questions in the form of simple sentences.

Dictionaries

A **dictionary** is a book of words.
A **dictionary** is a very useful book.
It helps you spell words.
It helps you find out what words mean.

Some **dictionaries** have pictures as well as words.

Words in **dictionaries** are in **alphabetical order**.
a b c d e f g h i j k l m n o p q r s t u v w x y z

Words that begin with the letter **a** are at the **front** of the book.

Words that begin with the letter **z** are at the **end** of the book.

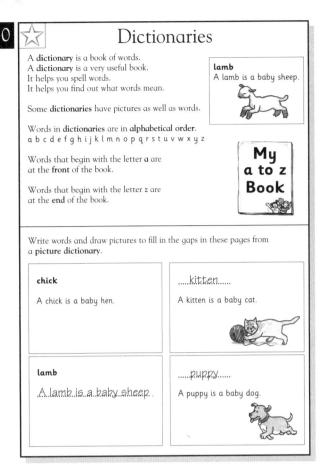

lamb
A lamb is a baby sheep.

My a to z Book

Write words and draw pictures to fill in the gaps in these pages from a **picture dictionary**.

chick
A chick is a baby hen.

...kitten......
A kitten is a baby cat.

lamb
A lamb is a baby sheep.

.....puppy......
A puppy is a baby dog.

Dictionaries help develop your child's reading and spelling skills. Explore and enjoy using them with your child. Help him or her to understand that words appear in alphabetical order and that this makes it easy to find specific entries.

Definitions

This is a **dictionary page** of **c** words. The words are in thick, **bold** letters.

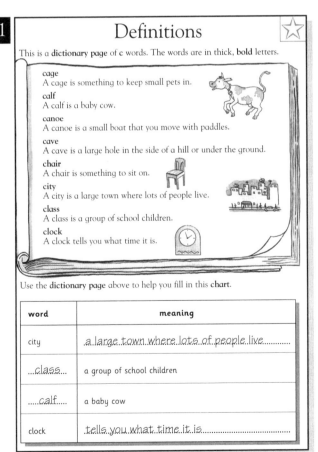

cage
A cage is something to keep small pets in.

calf
A calf is a baby cow.

canoe
A canoe is a small boat that you move with paddles.

cave
A cave is a large hole in the side of a hill or under the ground.

chair
A chair is something to sit on.

city
A city is a large town where lots of people live.

class
A class is a group of school children.

clock
A clock tells you what time it is.

Use the **dictionary page** above to help you fill in this **chart**.

word	meaning
city	a large town where lots of people live
class	a group of school children
calf	a baby cow
clock	tells you what time it is

Talk about and use dictionaries and word books with your child. Look at how words are located by their initial letters and then by subsequent letters. Use the word *definition* so that it becomes familiar, explaining that it gives the meaning of the word.

The or sound

Five spelling patterns make the same **or** sound. They are:
or as in for   oor as in door   ore as in store
aw as in raw   au as in taught

Write the missing letters to finish each word below. Then write the word on the line below.

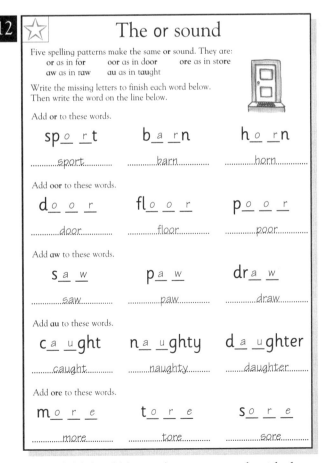

Add **or** to these words.

sp_o_ _r_t
..........sport..........

b_a_ _r_n
..........barn..........

h_o_ _r_n
..........horn..........

Add **oor** to these words.

d_o_ _o_ _r_
..........door..........

fl_o_ _o_ _r_
..........floor..........

p_o_ _o_ _r_
..........poor..........

Add **aw** to these words.

S_a_ _w_
..........saw..........

p_a_ _w_
..........paw..........

dr_a_ _w_
..........draw..........

Add **au** to these words.

c_a_ _u_ght
..........caught..........

n_a_ _u_ghty
..........naughty..........

d_a_ _u_ghter
..........daughter..........

Add **ore** to these words.

m_o_ _r_ _e_
..........more..........

t_o_ _r_ _e_
..........tore..........

s_o_ _r_ _e_
..........sore..........

Your child should know that many words with the same sound are spelled in different ways. This page offers your child lots of helpful practice in reading and spelling these same-sound words that have five different spelling patterns.

13 — Compound words

Some words are made up of two other words. When two short words make one long word, the long word is called a **compound word**.

Try these word sums. Write the two words without a space between them to make one **compound word**, like this: **head** + **rest** = **headrest**.

lamp	+ post	=	lamppost
her	+ self	=	herself
milk	+ man	=	milkman
hand	+ bag	=	handbag
foot	+ stool	=	footstool

Draw lines to join up these **compound words**.

foot — ball
him — self
post — card
pan — cake

play — ground
school — bag
post — man
tea — spoon

Now write a list of the **compound words** that you joined above.

football
himself
postcard
pancake

playground
schoolbag
postman
teaspoon

Help your child learn to split familiar compound words into their component parts, for example, *football* is made up of *foot* and *ball*. He or she may find it helpful to think of compound words and their component parts as simple sums.

14 — The er sound

Three spelling patterns make the same **er** sound. They are:
er as in **her**   **ir** as in **sir**   **ur** as in **fur**

Read these **er** sound words out loud.

sir   burn   skirt   her   purse   bird
turn   girl   hurt   shirt   curl   were

Now write the **ir** words on the shirt.

sir
shirt
skirt
bird
girl

Write the **ur** words in the purse.

purse
turn
hurt
burn
curl

Write the **er** words on the list.

her
were

Write **er** sound words to label these pictures.

Remember: The same sounds are spelled in different ways.

bird   skirt   nurse

This page offers activities that will help your child read and spell words that have the same *er* sound but different spelling patterns. Help your child to write the words as spelling-pattern sets and then to write words to match the picture clues.

15 — Syllables

Write your **first name** here. ....Answers may vary.......

How many **syllables** does your name have? ....Answers may vary.......

Remember: Each beat or unit in a word is called a **syllable**.

Write the **names** below on the **chart**.

Tom   Elizabeth   Lee   Natalie   Edward   Ben   Alexander
John   Amber   Mark   Sita   Tamara   Jenny   Kamal   Sunita

Remember: Names start with capital letters.

I syllable	2 syllables
Tom	Edward
Lee	Amber
Ben	Sita
John	Jenny
Mark	Kamal

3 syllables	4 syllables
Natalie	Elizabeth
Tamara	Alexander
Sunita	

I'm Kamal
I'm Amber
I'm Ben
I'm Sunita

Now write the number of **syllables** in the **months** of the year.

January	4	April	2	July	2	October	3
February	4	May	1	August	2	November	3
March	1	June	1	September	3	December	3

Help your child learn to discriminate and count the syllables in multi-syllabic words. You can also use the exercises on this page to help him or her practice writing proper names with capital letters and reading the months of the year.

16 — A traditional story

Read this **traditional story** out loud.

Chicken Licken

One day an acorn fell out of a tree and hit Chicken Licken.
    "The sky is falling!" she said. "I must go and tell the king."
    "Where are you going?" asked Henny Penny.
    "The sky is falling," said Chicken Licken. "A piece of it fell on me. I am going to tell the king."
    "I will go with you," said Henny Penny.

    Chicken Licken and Henny Penny met Cocky Locky.
    "Where are you going?" asked Cocky Locky.
    "The sky is falling," said Henny Penny. "Chicken Licken told me."
    "A piece of it fell on me," said Chicken Licken.
    "I will go with you," said Cocky Locky.

    Chicken Licken, Henny Penny and Cocky Locky met Ducky Daddles.
    "Where are you going?" asked Ducky Daddles.
    "The sky is falling," said Cocky Locky. "Henny Penny told me."
    "Chicken Licken told me," said Henny Penny.
    "A piece of it fell on me," said Chicken Licken.
    "I will go with you," said Ducky Daddles.

    Chicken Licken, Henny Penny, Cocky Locky and Ducky Daddles met Goosey Loosey, Turkey Lurkey and Foxy Woxy, too.
    "Run into my house," said Foxy Woxy. "You will be safe there. I will tell the king for you."

What did Foxy Woxy do next? Write the end of the **story**.
....................Answers may vary....................

Now tell the **story** in your own words.

This story will help your child towards confident independent reading through the repetition of key words, phrases and sentences. He or she should retell the story and use his or her understanding of it to predict events.

Punctuation

Speech marks show you when someone speaks.
Write **speech marks** like this " to show when speech **starts**.
Write speech marks like this " to show when speech **ends**.

"My name is Mark," said the boy.
The **speech marks** show what Mark said.

This is a **question mark**: ?
Put a **question mark** at the end of a sentence that asks a **question**.

"What is your name?" asked Mark.
The **question mark** shows that Mark asked a question.

This is an **exclamation mark**: !
Use it at the end of words or sentences to show **anger, surprise** or joy.

"Hi, Mark!" said Ben. "I'm Ben!"
The **exclamation marks** show that Ben was pleased.

Write sentences with **speech marks**, **question marks** and **exclamation marks**.
Remember to write who is speaking. The first sentence is done to show you how.

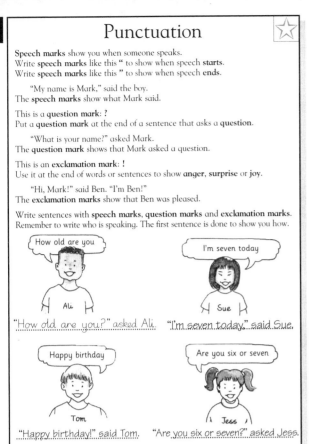

"How old are you?" asked Ali.   "I'm seven today." said Sue.

"Happy birthday!" said Tom.   "Are you six or seven?" asked Jess.

Your child needs to learn to identify speech marks, exclamation marks and question marks, to understand their purpose and to use them correctly. Help your child decide where to use each mark and rewrite the sentences.

Antonyms

An **antonym** is a word that has an **opposite** meaning to another word.
light is an **antonym** of **dark**
off is an **antonym** of **on**
Words can have more than one **antonym**.
How many **antonyms** for **big** can you think of? Write them here.

....

Draw lines to join the words that are **antonyms**.

back — last   few — empty
first — front   full — over
give — take   under — many

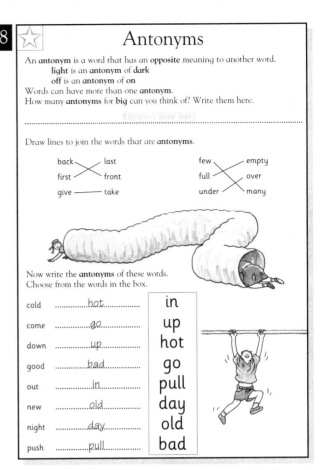

Now write the **antonyms** of these words.
Choose from the words in the box.

		box
cold	hot	in
come	go	up
down	up	hot
good	bad	go
out	in	pull
new	old	day
night	day	old
push	pull	bad

Talk about the word *antonym* with your child and explain that it signifies a word with a meaning that is opposite to another word. A word may have more than one antonym, for example, warm and hot are both antonyms of cold.

A poem to read

Read this **poem**. It is called *Busy Day* and is by a **poet** called Michael Rosen.

Busy Day

Pop in
pop out
pop over the road
pop out for a walk
pop in for a talk
pop down to the shop
can't stop
got to pop

got to pop?

pop where?
pop what?

well
I've got to
pop round
pop up
pop in to town
pop out and see
pop in for tea
pop down to the shop
can't stop
got to pop

gottapop?

pop where?
pop what?

well
I've got to
pop in
pop out
pop over the road
pop out for a walk
pop in for a talk ..

What is the **poem** about? Write a sentence.

....

Do you like the **poem** or not? Why?

....

Your child will enjoy reading this poem out loud. Encourage him or her to identify and talk about patterns of rhythm and rhyme and the repetition of words and phrases. He or she should form an opinion of the poem and give written reasons.

A traditional story

Read this **traditional story** from China. It is very old.

The Fox and the Raven

Once, long ago, a raven sat in a tree with some food in his beak.
    Along came a fox. He was hungry, and he wanted Raven's food.
    "Hello, Raven," said Fox. "My, what a fine bird you are!"
    Raven was pleased.
    "What shiny black feathers you have," said Fox. "How glossy they are!"
    Raven ruffled his feathers.
    "Raven, you really are the king of all the birds!" said Fox.
    Raven felt very proud.
    "I know what a wonderful voice you have," said Fox. "Will you let me hear you speak?"
    Raven was very pleased indeed. He opened his beak to speak – and dropped his food!
    Sly Fox picked it up and ate it. He laughed and laughed. "That will teach you a lesson, Raven," he said. "When someone tells you how wonderful you are, he may want something!"

Draw Fox under the tree. Write words for him to say in the speech bubble.

This page features a traditional Chinese story. Read and re-read it with your child, allowing more confident readers to read parts of it independently. Talk about the story, and ask your child to use his or her understanding of it to predict speech.

21 Words with ch and ph

The letters **ch** sometimes make the **ch** sound as in **ch**op. The letters **ch** can also make the hard **c** sound, as in **Ch**ris – the letter **h** is silent.

(Ring) the words below that have **ch** in them. Say them out loud.

"It's nearly (Christmas,") said (Christie.)

"I can't wait!" said (Nicholas.)

"It's a happy time," said (Christopher.)

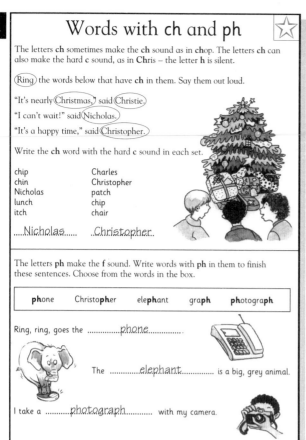

Write the **ch** word with the hard **c** sound in each set.

chip	Charles
chin	Christopher
Nicholas	patch
lunch	chip
itch	chair

.....Nicholas......   .Christopher.

The letters **ph** make the **f** sound. Write words with **ph** in them to finish these sentences. Choose from the words in the box.

phone	Christo**ph**er	ele**ph**ant	gra**ph**	**ph**otogra**ph**

Ring, ring, goes the ....phone...............

The ....elephant.............. is a big, grey animal.

I take a ....photograph........... with my camera.

On this page your child will learn that two letters together can make different sounds, for example *ch* can be hard as in *Ch*ristie and softer as in *ch*ip. Your child will also learn to recognise words where the letter *h* is silent.

22 A story to read

This is the first part of a **story** about a boy and a magic cat.

Marmaduke the Magic Cat
by Colin West

I often visit my grandma who lives on the other side of town. I like to help her out.

One day we were returning from the supermarket with the shopping. We were passing the library when we noticed a scruffy black cat ahead of us.

Instead of scampering away as we approached, the cat came right up and started rubbing against Grandma's leg, purring happily.

We couldn't resist stroking him. And what a funny cat he was.

His coat was bare in many places and his left ear was mauled as though he'd been in one scrap too many. He was wearing a bright tartan collar, and had a crooked little mouth which seemed to be curving into a smile.

The cat really loved being stroked, and soon Grandma bent down and started tickling him under the chin.

Grandma was enjoying it too. But after a while, she straightened up and said we should be making our way home.

But the cat had other ideas.

Your child will enjoy listening to this extract from a popular children's story. Read and re-read it together, and point to the words as you read them. If your child is a confident reader, he or she will be able to read the story independently.

23 Telling a story

Talk about the magic cat. What do you think might happen next in the **story**? Do you know any more cat stories? What are they called?

Write the name of the magic cat.

Marmalade

What colour was the magic cat?

black

Where did the boy and Grandma see the magic cat?

by the library

Write the words in the story that mean the same as the ones below.

fight	..........scrap...........	running	.........scampering.........
fur	...........coat...........	untidy	.........scruffy.........

Read the **story** to help you draw a picture of the magic cat. Write a **sentence** about him in your own words.

Answers may vary

Talk about what might happen next and about other cat stories your child may know. Help your child to use the text to answer the questions and to find synonyms. He or she will need to read carefully to identify clues that will help describe the cat.

24 Themed poems

Here are two **poems** to read.

Don't Call Alligator Long-mouth Till You Cross River
by John Agard

Call alligator long-mouth
call alligator saw-mouth
call alligator pushy-mouth
call alligator scissors-mouth
call alligator raggedy-mouth
call alligator bumpy-bum
call alligator all dem rude word
but better wait
     till you cross river.

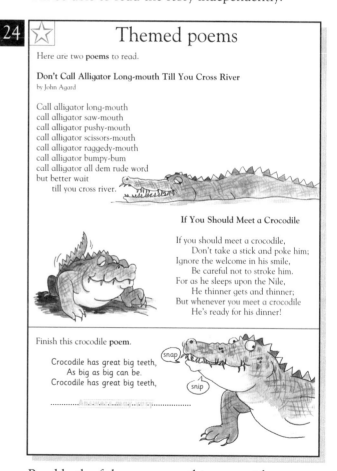

If You Should Meet a Crocodile

If you should meet a crocodile,
     Don't take a stick and poke him;
Ignore the welcome in his smile,
     Be careful not to stroke him.
For as he sleeps upon the Nile,
     He thinner gets and thinner;
But whenever you meet a crocodile
     He's ready for his dinner!

Finish this crocodile **poem**.

Crocodile has great big teeth,
     As big as big can be.
Crocodile has great big teeth,

...........Answers may vary...............

Read both of the poems on this page with your child, and talk about differences, similarities and elements of style. Ask your child to read the last poem independently and to supply a final line that rhymes.

Words with wh

The letters **wh** can make the **w** sound where the **h** is silent.

Write **wh** words to label these pictures. Choose from the words in the box.

white	wheat	whisk
whale	wheel	whistle

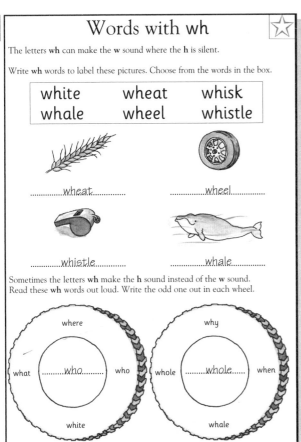

..........wheat..........   ....wheel..........

..........whistle..........   ....whale..........

Sometimes the letters **wh** make the **h** sound instead of the **w** sound.
Read these **wh** words out loud. Write the odd one out in each wheel.

where — what — ....who.......... — who — white

why — whole — ....whole...... — when — whale

Your child needs to recognise that two letters together can make different sounds when used in different words. The letters *wh* can make the *w* sound as in *wh*istle, where the *h* is silent, and the *h* sound as in *wh*ole, where the *w* is silent.

Prefixes

A **prefix** is a group of letters that is added to the beginning of a word. It changes the meaning of the word.
    un- is a **prefix**   **dis-** is a **prefix**

You can add the **prefix un-** to change the meaning of some words.
    un + load = unload   un + dress = undress

You can add the **prefix dis-** to change the meaning of other words.
    dis + obey = disobey

Add **un-** or **dis-** to the words in **bold** to finish the sentences below.   D

Jim **locks** the box.

Tim ....unlocks.......... it.

Nina **ties** her laces.

Kitty ....unties.......... them!

Yes, I **agree**.

No, I ....disagree...........

The toys are **tidy**.

The toys are ....untidy..........

Wes is **happy**.

Wes is ....unhappy..........

Explain the meaning of the term *prefix* to your child, and help him or her explore and understand that the effect of common prefixes such as *un-* and *dis-* is to change the meaning of positive words to negative words, such as *unhappy* or *displeased*.

Commas

A **comma** is a mark that is used to separate words. **Commas** separate words in lists. Look at the **commas** in the sentences below.

    Prem Ali Lucy Sam Jack and Aron are in my class. (without commas)
    Prem, Ali, Lucy, Sam, Jack and Aron are in my class. (with commas)

Write **commas** in these sentences.

I like to wear a T-shirt, shorts, cap and shoes.

Arms, legs, head, hands and feet are parts of the body.

Write **commas** in these sentences, then write the whole sentences with **commas**.

Sunday, Monday, Tuesday and Friday are days of the week.

Sunday, Monday, Tuesday and Friday are days of the week.

Red, blue, orange, green, yellow and purple are colours.

Red, blue, orange, green, yellow and purple are colours.

Write a sentence listing the names of some of the children in your class. Use **commas** in your sentence.

Remember: Names start with **capital letters.**

....
....
Answers may vary

Your child should be able to use punctuation marks in sentence construction with confidence and accuracy. He or she should understand how commas separate items in a list and be able to use them in sentences.

Grammar and accuracy

Finish each pair of sentences by choosing from the two **verbs** in the box.

I ....am.......... going to school.
Ben and Lisa ....are.......... going with me.
    | am are |

Today I ....feel.......... happy.
Last night I ....felt.......... sad.
    | felt feel |

Have you ....seen.......... the cartoon?
I ....saw.......... it last week.
    | saw seen |

Tick the sentences that are correct.

I were sad.	☐	We was at school.	☐
I went to town on the bus.	☑	We like riding our bikes.	☑
We were at school.	☑	I catched the ball.	☐
I go to the shop yesterday.	☐	I sayed hello to Peta.	☐

Finish each sentence by choosing from the words in the box.

Remember: Some words that sound the same have different meanings and spellings.

Let's go ....to.......... see the animals.
I can see ....two.......... monkeys.
I can see them, ...too.......... .
    | too / to / two |

Look, ...there..... are the seals.
They are having ....their..... dinner.
    | their / there |

I can ....hear..... the lions roaring.
..........Here..... they come!
    | here / hear |

Your child should develop the habit of checking his or her own written work for grammatical sense and accuracy, making corrections where necessary. Help him or her use appropriate verb tenses and learn the correct spellings of words that sound the same.

Descriptions

Read about Big Bad Bob.

Big Bad Bob has curly red hair and a big spot on the end of his nose.
He takes things that do not belong to him, and wears them.
He wears Grandma's fancy hat.
He wears Grandad's glasses.
He wears Mum's beads.
He wears my false beard.

Draw a picture of Big Bad Bob on the poster.

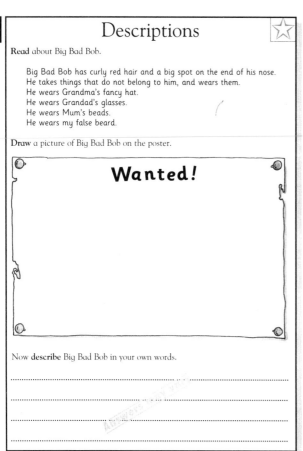

Wanted!

Now describe Big Bad Bob in your own words.

....
....
....
....

Encourage your child to read the text carefully,
with concentration, and to refer back to it to write
some appropriate words that describe Big Bad Bob.
Your child should also use information gained from
the text to produce an accurate drawing.

Glossaries

Some books have a list of words called a **glossary** at the back. A **glossary** tells
you what words mean, like a little **dictionary**. Read this glossary from a book
about plants.

flower	a part of a plant where new seeds grow
leaf	a part of a plant that grows on the stem
light	something plants need to grow
root	the part of a plant in the soil
seed	can grow into a new plant
seedling	a young plant
soil	the earth that plants grow in
stem	the main part of a plant
water	something plants need to grow

Now use the **glossary** above to write about plants.

A young plant is called a ...seedling.

What part of a plant is in the soil? ...root

What can grow into a new plant? ...seed

Write two things that plants need to grow...light..water

The words in a **glossary** are in **alphabetical order**. Tick the other things
below that have lists in **alphabetical order**.

class register ✔   book index ✔   story book ☐
comic ☐   telephone book ✔   atlas ✔

Discuss the features of non-fiction books with your
child. Look at a variety of examples at home or in
a library. Point out that a glossary is found at the
back of a book and that it defines difficult words.
Explain that the words are in alphabetical order.

Flow charts

A **flow chart** shows how something happens, how it is done or how it is made.
It shows the **order** of things. This **flow chart** shows how a plant grows.
Describe what happens in your own words.

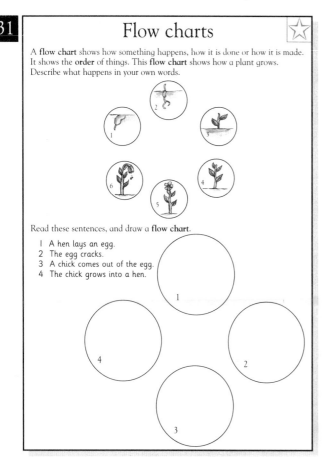

Read these sentences, and draw a **flow chart**.

1 A hen lays an egg.
2 The egg cracks.
3 A chick comes out of the egg.
4 The chick grows into a hen.

Explain that a flow chart is a diagrammatic way of
representing an activity, event or process and that it
can illustrate a sequence of events. Your child should
look at the flow chart and describe what it
represents, then draw pictures for another flow chart.

Personal information

Fill in this **form**.
Write about **yourself** and draw a picture.

name ....

address ....

....

postcode ....

Your date of birth is the day, month and year that you were born.

day .... **month** .... **year** ....

My date of birth is ....

Write about your **school**.

name ....

class ....

teacher ....

Now finish these sentences about **things you like doing**. Choose the right
words from the boxes.

I like	...reading...	redding	reading	reeding
I like	...writing...	writing	riting	ritting
I like	...spelling...	spilling	spelling	speling

The final page marks your child's completion of this
book. He or she should use it to record written
information about him- or herself, and details of his
or her school. The final activity focuses upon
developing reading, writing and spelling skills.

Punctuation

Speech marks show you when someone speaks.
Write **speech marks** like this " to show when speech **starts**.
Write **speech marks** like this " to show when speech **ends**.

"My name is Mark," said the boy.
The **speech marks** show what Mark said.

This is a **question mark**: ?
Put a **question mark** at the end of a sentence that asks a **question**.

"What is your name?" asked Mark.
The **question mark** shows that Mark asked a question.

This is an **exclamation mark**: !
Use it at the end of words or sentences to show **anger**, **surprise** or **joy**.

"Hi, Mark!" said Ben. "I'm Ben!"
The **exclamation marks** show that Ben was pleased.

Write sentences with **speech marks**, **question marks** and **exclamation marks**.
Remember to write who is speaking. The first sentence is done to show you how.

"How old are you?" asked Ali.

"I'm seven today" said Sue.

"Happy birthday" said Tom.

"Are you six or seven"? said Jess.

Antonyms

An **antonym** is a word that has an **opposite** meaning to another word.

> **light** is an **antonym** of **dark**
>
> **off** is an **antonym** of **on**

Words can have more than one **antonym**.

How many **antonyms** for **big** can you think of? Write them here.

....

Draw lines to join the words that are **antonyms**.

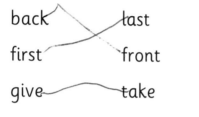

back	last		few	empty
first	front		full	over
give	take		under	many

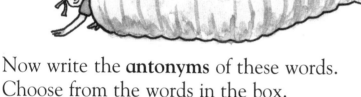

Now write the **antonyms** of these words.
Choose from the words in the box.

cold ...... hot

come ...... go

down ...... up

good ...... bad

out ...... in

new ...... old

night ...... day

push ...... pull

in ✓
up ✓
hot ✓
go ✓
pull ✓
day ✓
old ✓
bad ✓

A poem to read

Read this **poem**. It is called *Busy Day* and is by a **poet** called Michael Rosen.

Busy Day

Pop in
pop out
pop over the road
pop out for a walk
pop in for a talk
pop down to the shop
can't stop
got to pop

got to pop?

pop where?
pop what?

well
I've got to
pop round
pop up
pop in to town
pop out and see
pop in for tea
pop down to the shop
can't stop
got to pop

got to pop?

pop where?
pop what?

well
I've got to
pop in
pop out
pop over the road
pop out for a walk
pop in for a talk …

What is the **poem** about? Write a sentence.

. . . .

Do you like the **poem** or not? Why?

. . . .

A traditional story

Read this **traditional story** from China. It is very old.

The Fox and the Raven

Once, long ago, a raven sat in a tree with some food in his beak.

Along came a fox. He was hungry, and he wanted Raven's food.

"Hello, Raven," said Fox. "My, what a fine bird you are!"

Raven was pleased.

"What shiny black feathers you have," said Fox. "How glossy they are!"

Raven ruffled his feathers.

"Raven, you really are the king of all the birds!" said Fox.

Raven felt very proud.

"I know what a wonderful voice you have," said Fox. "Will you let me hear you speak?"

Raven was very pleased indeed. He opened his beak to speak – and dropped his food!

Sly Fox picked it up and ate it. He laughed and laughed. "That will teach you a lesson, Raven," he said. "When someone tells you how wonderful you are, he may want something!"

Draw Fox under the tree. Write words for him to say in the speech bubble.

Words with ch and ph

The letters **ch** sometimes make the **ch** sound as in **ch**op. The letters **ch** can also make the hard **c** sound, as in **Ch**ris – the letter **h** is silent.

(Ring) the words below that have **ch** in them. Say them out loud.

"It's nearly Christmas," said Christie.

"I can't wait!" said Nicholas.

"It's a happy time," said Christopher.

Write the **ch** word with the hard **c** sound in each set.

(chip)   (Charles)
(chin)   ⟩Christopher
Nicholas   (patch)
(lunch)   (chip)
(itch)   (chair)

...Nicholas......   ...Christopher...

The letters **ph** make the **f** sound. Write words with **ph** in them to finish these sentences. Choose from the words in the box.

phone	Christo**ph**er	ele**ph**ant	gra**ph**	**ph**otogra**ph**

Ring, ring, goes the ...phone................. .

The ...elephant................. is a big, grey animal.

I take a ...photograph................. with my camera.

A story to read

This is the first part of a **story** about a boy and a magic cat.

Marmaduke the Magic Cat
by Colin West

I often visit my grandma who lives on the other side of town. I like to help her out.

One day we were returning from the supermarket with the shopping. We were passing the library when we noticed a scruffy black cat ahead of us.

Instead of scampering away as we approached, the cat came right up and started rubbing against Grandma's leg, purring happily.

We couldn't resist stroking him. And what a funny cat he was.

His coat was bare in many places and his left ear was mauled as though he'd been in one scrap too many. He was wearing a bright tartan collar, and had a crooked little mouth which seemed to be curving into a smile.

The cat really loved being stroked, and soon Grandma bent down and started tickling him under the chin.

Grandma was enjoying it too. But after a while, she straightened up and said we should be making our way home.

But the cat had other ideas.

Telling a story

Talk about the magic cat. What do you think might happen next in the **story**? Do you know any more cat stories? What are they called?

Write the name of the magic cat.

....

What colour was the magic cat?

....

Where did the boy and Grandma see the magic cat?

....

Write the words in the story that mean the same as the ones below.

fight .... running ....

fur .... untidy ....

Read the **story** to help you draw a picture of the magic cat. Write a **sentence** about him in your own words.

Themed poems

Here are two **poems** to read.

Don't Call Alligator Long-mouth Till You Cross River
by John Agard

Call alligator long-mouth
call alligator saw-mouth
call alligator pushy-mouth
call alligator scissors-mouth
call alligator raggedy-mouth
call alligator bumpy-bum
call alligator all dem rude word
but better wait
      till you cross river.

If You Should Meet a Crocodile

If you should meet a crocodile,
    Don't take a stick and poke him;
Ignore the welcome in his smile,
    Be careful not to stroke him.
For as he sleeps upon the Nile,
    He thinner gets and thinner;
But whenever you meet a crocodile
    He's ready for his dinner!

Finish this crocodile **poem**.

  Crocodile has great big teeth,
    As big as big can be.
  Crocodile has great big teeth,

....

snap

snip

Words with wh

The letters **wh** can make the **w** sound where the **h** is silent.

Write **wh** words to label these pictures. Choose from the words in the box.

white	wheat	whisk
whale	wheel	whistle

....

....

Sometimes the letters **wh** make the **h** sound instead of the **w** sound.
Read these **wh** words out loud. Write the odd one out in each wheel.

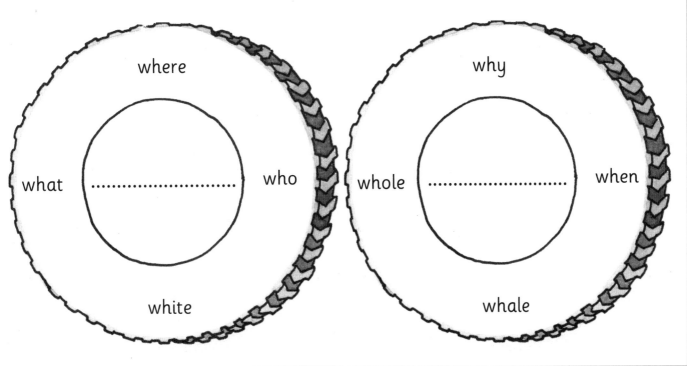

Prefixes

A **prefix** is a group of letters that is added to the beginning of a word.
It changes the meaning of the word.

    un- is a **prefix**   **dis-** is a **prefix**

You can add the **prefix un-** to change the meaning of some words.
    un + load = unload   un + dress = undress

You can add the **prefix dis-** to change the meaning of other words.
    dis + obey = disobey

Add **un-** or **dis-** to the words in **bold** to finish the sentences below. | D |

Jim **locks** the box.

Tim .... it.

Nina **ties** her laces.

Kitty .... them!

Yes, I **agree**.

No, I ....

The toys are **tidy**.

The toys are ....

Wes is **happy**.

Wes is ....

Commas

A **comma** is a mark that is used to separate words. **Commas** separate words in lists. Look at the **commas** in the sentences below.

Prem Ali Lucy Sam Jack and Aron are in my class. (without commas)
Prem, Ali, Lucy, Sam, Jack and Aron are in my class. (with commas)

Write **commas** in these sentences.

I like to wear a T-shirt shorts cap and shoes.

Arms legs head hands and feet are parts of the body.

Write **commas** in these sentences, then write the whole sentences with **commas**.

Sunday Monday Tuesday and Friday are days of the week.

....

....

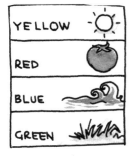

Red blue orange green yellow and purple are colours.

....

....

Write a sentence listing the names of some of the children in your class.
Use **commas** in your sentence.

Remember: Names start with **capital letters**.

....

....

Grammar and accuracy

Finish each pair of sentences by choosing from the two **verbs** in the box.

I .... *am* .... going to school.

Ben and Lisa .... *are* .... going with me.

| am are |

Today I .... *feel* .... happy.

Last night I .... *felt* .... sad.

| felt feel |

Have you .... *seen* .... the cartoon?

I .... *saw* .... it last week.

| saw seen |

Tick the sentences that are correct.

I were sad. ☒

I went to town on the bus. ☑

We were at school. ☑

I go to the shop yesterday. ☒

We was at school. ☒

We like riding our bikes. ☑

I catched the ball. ☒

I sayed hello to Peta. ☒

Finish each sentence by choosing from the words in the box.

Remember: Some words that sound the same have different meanings and spellings.

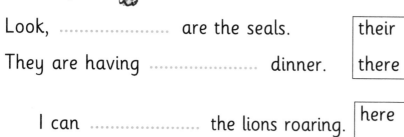

Let's go .... *to* .... see the animals.

I can see .... *two* .... monkeys.

I can see them, ... *two* ....

| too |
| to |
| two |

Look, ... are the seals.

They are having .... dinner.

| their |
| there |

I can .... the lions roaring.

.... they come!

| here |
| hear |

Descriptions

Read about Big Bad Bob.

> Big Bad Bob has curly red hair and a big spot on the end of his nose.
> He takes things that do not belong to him, and wears them.
> He wears Grandma's fancy hat.
> He wears Grandad's glasses.
> He wears Mum's beads.
> He wears my false beard.

Draw a picture of Big Bad Bob on the poster.

Now **describe** Big Bad Bob in your own words.

~~Big Bad Bob Wears~~ Big Bad Bob wears
My skirt, wears my top, wears my
tights and shoes.

Glossaries

Some books have a list of words called a **glossary** at the back. A **glossary** tells you what words mean, like a little **dictionary**. Read this **glossary** from a book about plants.

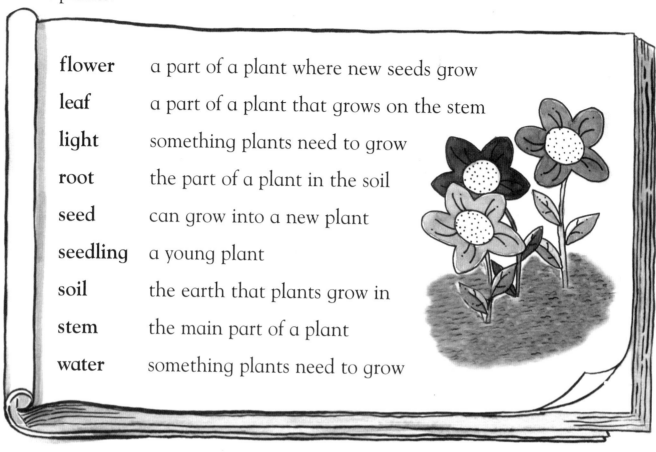

flower	a part of a plant where new seeds grow
leaf	a part of a plant that grows on the stem
light	something plants need to grow
root	the part of a plant in the soil
seed	can grow into a new plant
seedling	a young plant
soil	the earth that plants grow in
stem	the main part of a plant
water	something plants need to grow

Now use the **glossary** above to write about plants.

A young plant is called a ..... *Seedling* .....

What part of a plant is in the soil? *root*

What do new plants grow from? *Seed*

What can grow into a new plant? *flower*

The words in a **glossary** are in **alphabetical order**. Tick the other things below that have lists in **alphabetical order**.

class register ☑   book index ☑   story book ☐

comic ☒   telephone book ☑   atlas ☑

Flow charts

A **flow chart** shows how something happens, how it is done or how it is made. It shows the **order** of things. This **flow chart** shows how a plant grows. Describe what happens in your own words.

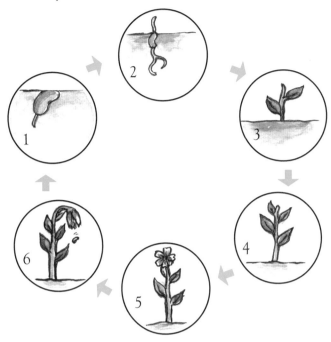

Read these sentences, and draw a **flow chart**.

1 A hen lays an egg.
2 The egg cracks.
3 A chick comes out of the egg.
4 The chick grows into a hen.

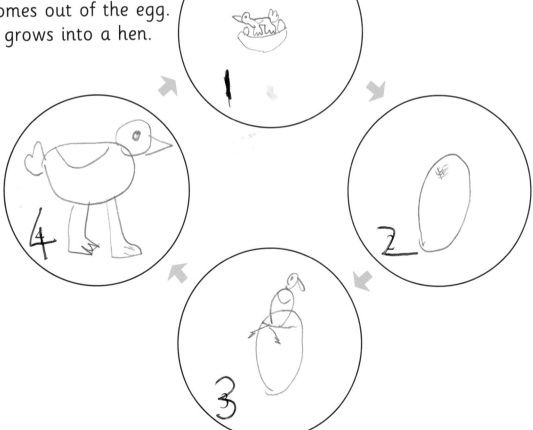

Personal information

Fill in this **form**.
Write about **yourself** and draw a picture.

name Rebecca Hardy

address 7 Beechwood Ave. Richmond

Surrey

postcode TW9 4dd

Your date of birth is the day, month and year that you were born.

day sunday **month** march **year** 1996

My date of birth is 3rd march

Write about your **school**.

name Rebecca Hardy

class 2M

teacher mrs Austin

Now finish these sentences about **things you like doing**. Choose the right
words from the boxes.

I like reading

I like writing

I like Spelling

redding	reading	reeding
writing	riting	ritting
spilling	spelling	speling